WHAT WERE YOU IN A PREVIOUS LIFE?

BY ADAM GREEN

 THUNDER'S MOUTH PRESS

PUBLISHED BY THUNDER'S MOUTH PRESS
632 BROADWAY, 7TH FLOOR
NEW YORK, NEW YORK 10012

ISBN 1-56025-068-2
1-56025-069-0 (8-COPY PREPACK)

LCN 93-60863

SOME OF THESE CARTOONS WERE PREVIOUSLY PUBLISHED BY PARANORMAL PRESS UNDER THE TITLE, "CRAZY STRAWS AND BROKEN HEARTS"

THANKS ARE DUE FOR PERMISSION TO QUOTE FROM THE FOLLOWING COPYRIGHTED SOURCES: FOR A PASSAGE OF "NEW YEARS EVE" FROM "IN DREAMS BEGIN RESPONSIBILITIES AND OTHER STORIES" BY DELMORE SCHWARTZ, COPYRIGHT © 1948, 1961 BY DELMORE SCHWARTZ, REPRINTED BY PERMISSION OF NEW DIRECTIONS PUBLISHING CORP.; FOR A PASSAGE FROM "STREET HASSLE PART II" FROM "BETWEEN THOUGHT AND EXPRESSION SELECTED LYRICS OF LOU REED" COPYRIGHT © 1991 METAL MACHINE MUSIC INC., REPRINTED BY PERMISSION OF HYPERION A DIVISION OF DISNEY PUBLISHING COMPANY, INC.

SPECIAL THANKS TO: ERIN, ADINA, MILDRED, AND BENJAMIN; JOHN AND BARBARA AT THE CHICAGO TRIBUNE; NEIL, REBECCA, JOSEPH, AND CHERIE AT THUNDER'S MOUTH PRESS; MARK, AND TIM AT PUBLISHERS GROUP WEST; BERKELEY, BILL, AND LOU FOR THE BACK COVER WORDS; FRIENDS, AND LOVERS; PEOPLE WHO HAVE BEEN NICE IN PASSING; ANYONE WHO BUYS THIS BOOK; AND ANYONE I MIGHT HAVE LEFT OUT (SORRY)...

DISTRIBUTED BY PUBLISHERS GROUP WEST
4065 HOLLIS STREET
EMERYVILLE, CALIFORNIA 94608
1-800-788-3123

SEXUAL QUIRKS OF FICTIONAL CHARACTERS #17: THE MUSIC MAN

THINGS NOT TO SAY WHILE DRIVING BACK FROM YOUR GRANDFATHER'S FUNERAL, AFTER YOUR SISTER RUNS OVER A RACCOON

DESPERATE PLAYS FOR ATTENTION (AT A ROUND TABLE)

LUSTFUL PLAYS ON A BIG BLACK COUCH IN THE FACE OF APOCALYPSE . . .

SAFETY TIP#7: WHEN LOOKING DIRECTLY INTO A NUCLEAR BLAST, IT IS BEST TO SPORT PROTECTIVE EYEWEAR . . .

QUARTET OF REJECTION

WELL, I SEE IT IN A SORT OF MULTI-CULTURAL, MINIMALIST, NEO, POST, ABSTRACT, MODERN, KINETIC, PRIMITIVE... SORT OF WAY...
HIGH-BROW HOOTCH
YES, YES, YES, AND I CAN TOUCH MY TONGUE TO MY NOSE... WOULD YOU LIKE A TWINKIE?

WHY ONE SHOULD TAKE EXTREME CARE WHEN TYING ONE'S DOG TO A POST...

I had no intention of becomin' another run-of-the-mill, ball-peen-hammer-wielding-psycho... But one day the angels and devils in mah head that were ah disgreein', started agreein'...
KILL KILL KILL
KILL KILL KILL
GOD SAYS IT'S O.K..
SATAN GIVES YOU THE BIG "THUMBS UP!"
Adam 92
© 1992 ADAM GREEN

IF YOU WERE INDEPENDENTLY WEALTHY AND COULD DO ANYTHING YOU WANTED, WHAT WOULD YOU DO?

ONE TO ONE WE'RE ALL CONNECTED...

A BITTER LITTLE POSTCARD FROM A BITTER LITTLE MAN

NASTINESS IS A TORN PUPPY

PERFORMANCE ART GUYS

HOW NOT TO ORDER MONGOLIAN BEEF

LITTLE KNOWN SOCIAL ILLS #23: THE ILLITERACY OF LAB ANIMALS

IT'S THE ATTITUDE, NOT THE CIRCUMSTANCES

FAILED MONEY-MAKING SCHEMES #31: NOVELTY BABY BIBS...

PHRASES ELVIS PRESLEY USED, THAT YOU CAN USE IN EVERYDAY CONVERSATION

THE PERSON IS POLITICAL

UNSUCCESSFUL WAYS TO DEAL WITH YOUR PROBLEMS #13: DRUGS AND FLEEING

MARRY ME! FOR I AM THE FROG PRINCE AND THESE ARE MY TADPOLE BROTHERS!
MY WHOLE LIFE JUST SUCKS...
90

NIGHTMARE ON SESAME STREET

P H O B I A S

GNOME-O-PHOBIA
NOW DON'T FORGET TO CHECK UNDER THE BED FOR LITTLE PEOPLE
O.K.
FOAM-O-PHOBIA
I CAN ONLY USE FEATHER PILLOWS
O.K.
MOAN-O-PHOBIA
I CAN'T HAVE SEX
O.K.
CLONE-O-PHOBIA
DO I LOOK O.K. I CAN'T LOOK IN A MIRROR
O.K.
HOME-O-PHOBIA
DO YOU THINK IT'S TRUE, YOU CAN'T GO HOME AGAIN?
O.K.
HOME AWAY FROM HOME-O-PHOBIA
I CAN'T BE COMFORTABLE ANYWHERE!
O.K.
ROLLING STONE-O-PHOBIA
DON'T EVEN PLAY A MICK JAGGER SOLO RECORD
O.K.
ROLLING STONE-AWAY FROM HOME-O-PHOBIA
WHAT IF MICK JAGGER ISN'T EVEN IN HIS HOUSE RIGHT NOW?
ROLLING STONE WITH ANOTHER ROLLING STONE - AWAY FROM HOME-O-PHOBIA
WHAT IF HE AND KEITH . . . ? WHAT WOULD JERRY SAY?

THERE ARE SOME TRICKS YOU CAN'T TEACH EVEN A NEW DOG

A MOMENT OF HESITATION

EXCERPT FROM DATE THIRTY SEVEN

WHAT IF MARKY MARK WASN'T A FAMOUS RAPPER?

CONTRARY TO WHAT IS IMPLIED FROM TELEVISION, YOU CANNOT REACH WILLIAM SHATNER BY DIALING 9-1-1

BREAKFAST FOOD ANALYZED

WARNING SIGNS THAT MIGHT INDICATE THAT YOU OR YOUR FAMILY AND FRIENDS ARE DRIFTING TOWARD SATANISM

ZEN AND THE ART OF TOTAL PSYCHOSIS (A REAL LIFE ADVENTURE

DOG DAY AFTERNOON

SCENES FROM A DYSFUNCTIONAL RELATIONSHIP #17: THE BEDROOM

YET ANOTHER REASON NOT TO WEAR EXPENSIVE GARMENTS MADE FROM THE PIECES OF ADORABLE LITTLE FUZZY ANIMALS DESTROYED FOR YOUR VANITY

THE CALM BEFORE THE STORM

SPIDERMAN CONFESSES

UMMM...WELL...I EAT BUGS! O.K.?!?
THERE, I SAID IT... IS THAT SO WRONG?
I MEAN, I USED TO BE A PIMPLY-FACED, BED-
WETTING, SCIENCE GEEK UNTIL I WAS BITTEN
BY A RADIOACTIVE SPIDER... AND NOW I'M
LIKE A SUPER-HERO THAT COULD RIP YOUR
HEAD OFF... SO I'M NOT THE ONE WITH
THE PROBLEM,
WUSSY-BOY!

© 1993 ADAM "SLOUCHY CARTOON GEEK" GREEN

Adam 93

THERE ARE ONLY TWO THINGS IN THIS WORLD YOU CAN BE CERTAIN OF: DEATH AND TAXIS (TRUE-LIFE CAB CONVERSATIONS #3)

EARTH ANGEL

EDWARD LIZARD HANDS

IT AIN'T WHAT YOU DO, IT'S THE WAY THAT YOU DO IT...

THINGS NOT TO INFLATE WITH A BICYCLE PUMP #3: YOUR PET

BAD DAY AT THE GUIDANCE COUNSELOR'S OFFICE...

THE ART OF IRRESPONSIBILITY

I WALKED WITH A ZOMBIE

WHY LEARNING PASSIVE RESISTANCE IS SUCH A TRICKY BUSINESS . . .

MOMMY, ARE THERE MONSTERS UNDER MY BED?
OH NO! THOSE ARE JUST REALLY BIG SNAKES... THE MONSTERS ARE IN YOUR UNDERWEAR DRAWER...
Adam 93
©1993 ADAM "MY MOTHER EATS MONSTERS FOR BREAKFAST" GREEN

HOUND OF LOVE

SPECIAL LIFE MOMENTS #13: THE INSTANT YOU REALIZE THAT ALL OF YOUR FRIENDS HAVE BEEN SLEEPING WITH ALL OF YOUR OTHER FRIENDS (FOR A VERY LONG TIME)

PORTRAIT OF A YOUNG MALE NEUROTIC DANCER...

HOW TO RELATE BETTER TO YOUR CAT

THE REAL REASON PEOPLE BUY CAR PHONES . . .

GRAVITY BOOT CONFESSIONS

TERRIBLE PHONE FACTS #3

BAD DAY THROUGH THE LOOKING GLASS

RAINY DAY FUN ACTIVITY # 7: MAKE EXOSKELETONS OUT OF OLD BLEACH BOTTLES

WHY I DON'T DRAW THE SPECTACULAR AMAZING SPIDERMAN FOR A LIVING

I'M JUST NOT WORTHY.

I HATE THAT.

IT WOULD CUT INTO MY TIME CURRENTLY SPENT TEACHING CHIMPANZEES TO SPEAK...

HUH?

I BECOME SO ENTHRALLED BY THE STORIES, MY PALMS SWEAT, I CAN'T HOLD A PEN, AND I NEED TO URINATE...

I KILLED SPIDER-MAN!

IN REAL, ACTUAL LIFE I AM THE MIGHTY THOR! (AND IT WOULD BE A MAJOR CONFLICT OF INTEREST)

TA-DA!

COUGH SPUT COUGH

Adam 92

MICHAEL JACKSON EXPLAINS HIMSELF...

WELL, WHEN I TOUCH MYSELF HERE I'M NOT TOUCHING ME ... I'M TOUCHING A UNIVERSAL SPIRIT OF LOVE FOR ALL THE CHILDREN ON THIS PLANET AND OTHERS...

Adam 93

ANOTHER REASON NOT TO GO OUT WITH PSYCHOPATHS: IT'S OFTEN MESSY...

YET ANOTHER CARTOON THAT FAILS TO ADDRESS CLASS STRUGGLE (A.K.A. "CHOP GOES THE WEASEL"

SOMETIMES YOU JUST CAN'T TRUST PLASTIC TOYS TO PREDICT THE FUTURE...

MY BI-WEEKLY PHONE CONVERSATION WITH MY SISTER . . .

WHAT KIND OF TATTOO WOULD YOU GET AND WHERE WOULD IT BE?

OBSESSION EXPLAINED

DEATH · DISEASE
ENNUI · MONEY
ANGST · GLOOM
EXCESSIVE TARTAR BUILD-UP
CONSPIRACY THEORIES · MADONNA

YOU · YOU · YOU
YOU · YOU · YOU
YOU · YOU · YOU
YOU · YOU · YOU · YOU

BEFORE

AFTER

About the Author

PHOTO BY M. GREEN

ADAM GREEN'S CARTOONS HAVE APPEARED IN:
THE CHICAGO TRIBUNE, THE UTNE READER,
THE SAN FRANCISCO BAY GUARDIAN, AND NUMEROUS
OTHER PUBLICATIONS.

HE LIVES WITH THE CONSTANT FEAR THAT ONE
DAY A GROUP OF ATTRACTIVE VAMPIRES WILL
SPIRIT HIM AWAY TO A SCENIC CASTLE IN SPAIN,
BRING HIM TO MANY AN INTENSE ORGASM, THEN
RIP HIS STOMACH OPEN LIKE A CHEAP BAG OF
POTATO CHIPS, MAKING GROTESQUE "BALLOON
ANIMALS" OUT OF HIS SMALL INTESTINE...

BEFORE THIS INEVITABLE EVENT, HE ENCOURAGES
YOU TO BUY EXTRA COPIES OF THIS BOOK, OR
ORIGINAL ARTWORK FROM IT... SEND LETTERS
OF PRAISE, QUERIES, GIFTS, WHATEVER C/O:
THUNDER'S MOUTH PRESS, 632 BROADWAY,
7TH FLOOR, NEW YORK, NY 10012